SUPER
SANDCASTLE™
It's the Alphabet!

It's W!

Mary Elizabeth Salzmann

Consulting Editor, Diane Craig, M.A./Reading Specialist

ABDO
Publishing Company

Published by ABDO Publishing Company, 8000 West 78th Street, Edina, Minnesota 55439. Copyright © 2010 by Abdo Consulting Group, Inc. International copyrights reserved in all countries. No part of this book may be reproduced in any form without written permission from the publisher. Super SandCastle™ is a trademark and logo of ABDO Publishing Company.

Printed in the United States.

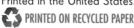 PRINTED ON RECYCLED PAPER

Editor: Katherine Hengel
Content Developer: Nancy Tuminelly
Cover and Interior Design and Production: Kelly Doudna, Mighty Media
Photo Credits: iStockphoto (Jani Bryson, Shantell), Shutterstock

Library of Congress Cataloging-in-Publication Data
Salzmann, Mary Elizabeth, 1968-
  It's W! / Mary Elizabeth Salzmann.
    p. cm. -- (It's the alphabet!)
  ISBN 978-1-60453-610-2
  1. English language--Alphabet--Juvenile literature. 2. Alphabet books--Juvenile literature. I. Title.
  PE1155.S2695 2010
  421'.1--dc22
  ⟨E⟩
                                    2009022177

JEASY
ITS

Super SandCastle™ books are created by a team of professional educators, reading specialists, and content developers around five essential components—phonemic awareness, phonics, vocabulary, text comprehension, and fluency—to assist young readers as they develop reading skills and strategies and increase their general knowledge. All books are written, reviewed, and leveled for guided reading, early reading intervention, and Accelerated Reader® programs for use in shared, guided, and independent reading and writing activities to support a balanced approach to literacy instruction.

About SUPER SANDCASTLE™

Bigger Books for Emerging Readers
Grades K–4

Created for library, classroom, and at-home use, Super SandCastle™ books support and engage young readers as they develop and build literacy skills and will increase their general knowledge about the world around them. Super SandCastle™ books are an extension of SandCastle™, the leading preK–3 imprint for emerging and beginning readers. Super SandCastle™ features a larger trim size for more reading fun.

Let Us Know
Super SandCastle™ would like to hear your stories about reading this book. What was your favorite page? Was there something hard that you needed help with? Share the ups and downs of learning to read. We want to hear from you! Send us an e-mail.

sandcastle@abdopublishing.com

Contact us for a complete list of SandCastle™, Super SandCastle™, and other nonfiction and fiction titles from ABDO Publishing Company.

www.abdopublishing.com • 8000 West 78th Street
Edina, MN 55439 • 800-800-1312 • 952-831-1632 fax

3/26/11

$17.95

Aa Bb Cc Dd Ee
Ff Gg Hh Ii Jj Kk
Ll Mm Nn Oo Pp
Qq Rr Ss Tt Uu Vv
Ww Xx Yy Zz

The Letter Ww

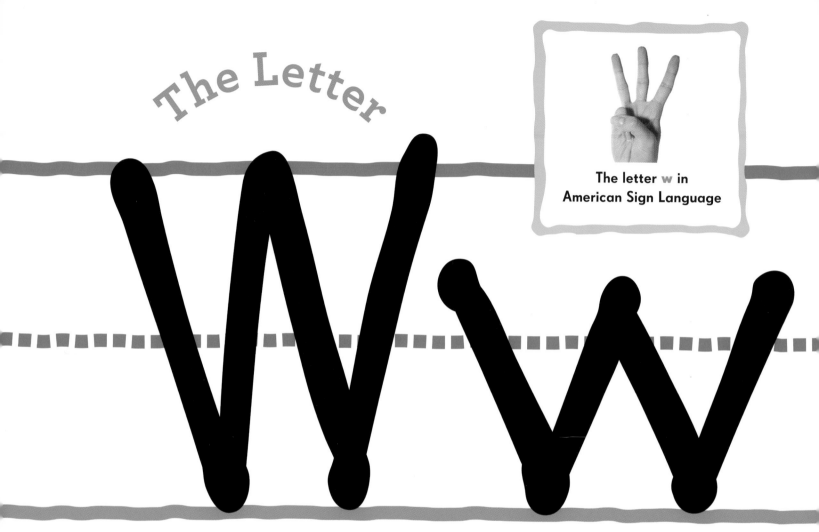

The letter w in American Sign Language

W and w can also look like

Ww **Ww** Ww Ww Ww Ww

The letter w is a consonant.

It is the 23rd letter of the alphabet.

☞ Some words start with **w**.

well

walrus

Wyatt

On Wednesdays, Wyatt waits at the well to watch the walrus walk by.

Some words have **w** in the middle.

clown

owl

flowers

8

Gwen

Gwen owes twelve flowers to the clown sitting down between two brown owls.

Some words have **w** at the end.

cow

scarecrow

arrow

Drew saw a cow follow the arrow around the yellow scarecrow.

Drew

11

wh as in **while**

whale

wheat

wheelbarrow

Whitney

No words end with wh.

Whitney whispers to her whale while going nowhere in a wheelbarrow full of wheat.

Way down below a wild ocean wave,
Willis the whale swims up to a white cave.

Willis sees a sign that warns,
"Watch Out!"

But he wonders,
"What do I have to worry about?"

With that, Willis wiggles
his tail and swims inside.

"Wow!" Willis thinks.
"This cave is not very wide!"

WATCH OUT!

17

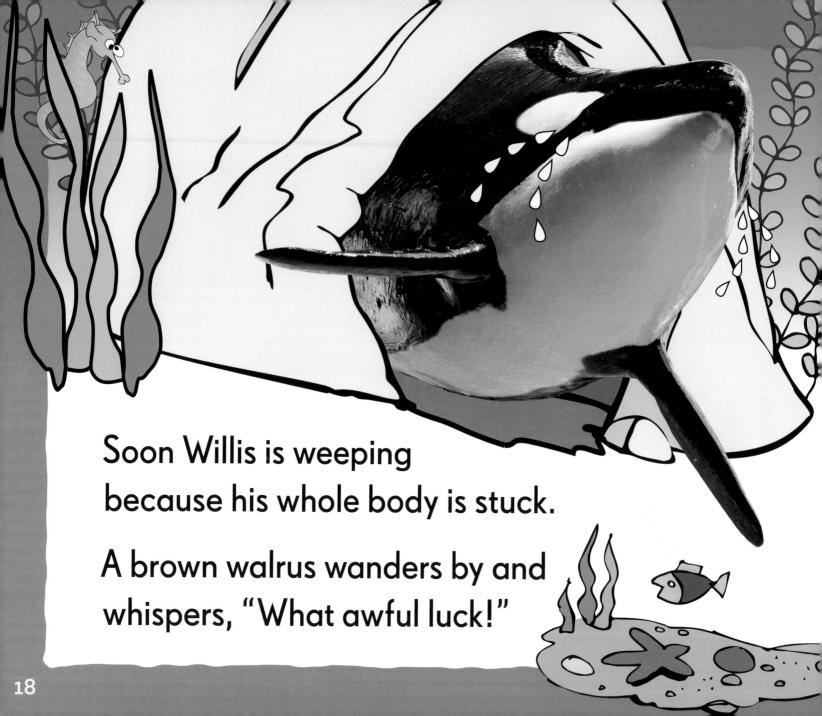

Soon Willis is weeping
because his whole body is stuck.

A brown walrus wanders by and
whispers, "What awful luck!"

"Whoa! Wait!" Willis wails.
"Would you please help me?"

Wanda the walrus says,
"Don't worry. I'll work to set you free!"

Wanda wraps yellow seaweed around Willis and pulls him right out.

"I owe you!" says Willis. "You're the wisest walrus without a doubt!"

Which words have
the letter **w**?

whale

well

owl

ladybug

rock

walrus

scarecrow

squirrel

Glossary

awful (p. 18) – very bad.

owe (pp. 9, 20) – to need to pay someone for something or return a favor.

seaweed (p. 20) – a plant that grows in the ocean.

wail (p. 19) – to make a long cry of sadness or pain.

warn (p. 16) – to tell someone that something bad could happen.

weep (p. 18) – to cry.

wheelbarrow (pp. 12, 13) – a cart with two handles and one wheel.

whoa (p. 19) – a word used to tell a horse or another animal to stop.

wiggle (p. 17) – to move back and forth quickly.

wrap (p. 20) – to wind something around a person or object.

To promote letter recognition, letters are highlighted instead of glossary words in this series. The page numbers above indicate where the glossary words can be found.

More Words with **W**

Find the **w** in the beginning, middle, or end of each word.

always	how	snow	we	winter
answer	low	sweet	week	witch
away	new	town	wet	woman
draw	now	wall	who	word
few	own	walnut	why	worm
grow	row	water	will	write